Fifty-Two Weeks
of Journaling Through Child Loss

AMANDA HARTWIG

ten16press.com - Waukesha, WI

Fifty-Two Weeks of Journaling Through Child Loss
Copyright © 2020 Amanda Hartwig

Fifty-Two Weeks of Journaling Through Child Loss
by Amanda Hartwig
ISBN 978-1-64538-256-0

All Rights Reserved. Written permission must be secured from the publisher to use or reproduce any part of this book, except for brief quotations in critical reviews or articles.

For information, please contact:

ten16press.com
Waukesha, WI

Illustrated by Sara Bastian

Hello dear friend,

My name is Amanda Hartwig, and I am President and Founder of Bo's Heavenly Clubhouse. We are a nonprofit charity organization that is dedicated to helping parents with the death of their child. A charity organization that is always open. I am a wife to an amazing husband who works incredibly hard for his family, and a mother to three beautiful children, Ari, Bo, and River. Bo died when he was ten months old from the adenovirus, otherwise known as the common cold. In my years of service to the child loss community and in collaboration with Bo's Heavenly Clubhouse, I have been the one on the other line of the phone that people call in their desperate moments. I have personally assembled over 300 care packages since our founding in 2016. These care packages consist of child loss books, Bibles, journals, coloring books, pens and pencils, stress balls, and other various child loss aids. We also help with funeral expenses for children who are eighteen years old and younger throughout the state of Wisconsin. Additionally, my husband Wayne and I host child loss support groups in our local area of Wisconsin to further help deliver child loss families from their pits of despair. We give them a safe place to vent, learn, and listen.

This book is designed to help get you through the first year of child loss. You and I will walk alongside each other in our most vulnerable moments. You will not ever get OVER your child being gone. That is not possible. The pain never goes away. Over time, you just learn to wear it better.

Grief takes work, LOTS of work. Before embarking on this journey to healing, I must ask you one question. Are you willing to put in the effort that it takes? The essential effort to crawl out of the tunnel of despair. The endless black pit that holds all of us as child loss survivors in the grips of hopelessness and agony. Are you willing to dedicate a few minutes per week to yourself and your heart? Because that's the ultimate sacrifice. Putting aside warranted time where you can roll up your sleeves and get to work. If you do this journal to the designated completion, I promise that by the end of this, you will have put in more effort and work towards your own personal walk with child loss grief than you did before you found this.

Dealing with my own loss from the death of my beloved ten-month-old son Bo, I have found a way to turn back around and help the ones that are newly grieving on this excruciatingly painful road of child loss. To return to the pits of hell with buckets of water and to try to pour out other's fires, to help them, to let them know that they are not alone.

Whoever gifted you this journal just wants to help you. They probably don't know quite what to say and maybe feel like there's not much else that they can do at this point. And they're right. They can't do anything but be there. But if this is a gift from someone, just know that they love you so very much and that they deserve grace right now. Yes, I know that your child just died, but they are doing the best that they can to be a support to you, while watching helplessly as you suffer in agony. Let this gift from them show how much they love you.

Let's get started.

I'm so sorry that you're here in this moment right now, with me. I don't want you here any more than you want to be here. This is a group that no one wants to be a part of. But we're in this together. There's strength in numbers. That is why this first journal prompt is something that seems "simple," but right now, it's so important. It is so important for that mama or daddy heart of yours.

SAY. THEIR. NAME.
Write it down and then write it again.
Because your child was here, because they existed.
*Because death **does not** negate existence.*

REMEMBER THIS WEEK
Through the tears that you have been crying, your body needs water. Even if you don't have your appetite, make sure to try to drink water. When you think you've had enough, drink another glass.

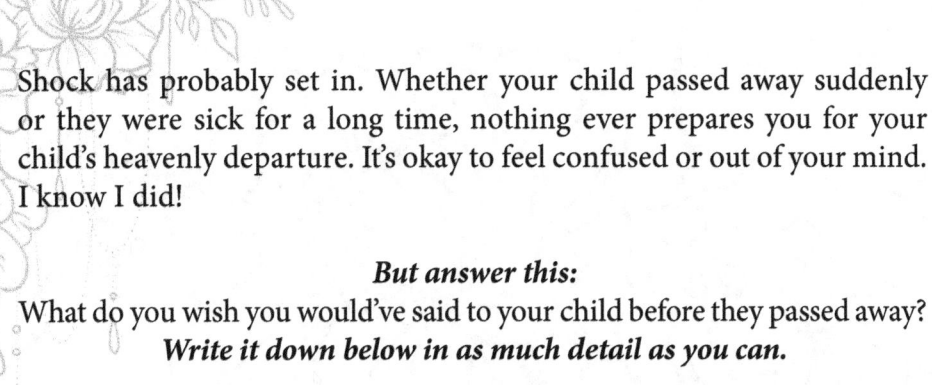

Shock has probably set in. Whether your child passed away suddenly or they were sick for a long time, nothing ever prepares you for your child's heavenly departure. It's okay to feel confused or out of your mind. I know I did!

But answer this:
What do you wish you would've said to your child before they passed away?
Write it down below in as much detail as you can.

_____
_____
_____
_____
_____
_____
_____
_____
_____
_____
_____
_____

REMEMBER THIS WEEK
Try to eat something. Even if it is cheese and crackers. Eat a little something.

When child loss happens, we tend to "live" in the past, a time when our beloved child was alive. So, for this week, list the happiest moments that you were gifted with them. That's right, this is permission to go back to the past and relive some of your fondest memories. ***List them below:***

-
-
-
-
-
-
-
-
-
-
-

REMEMBER THIS WEEK

Grief can overwhelm every aspect of our lives. Make sure to come back to this list every day that you can. Recall these memories and breathe. Take long, slow, deep breaths.

The anger is real and probably undeniable at this point. It is so easy to get caught up in the feelings of grief. To acknowledge the anger is to acknowledge the pain. The anger will be here for a while, and we need to deal with it properly. It may be tempting to bury it, along with the rest of your feelings. But I would caution you to not do that. You've been given this workbook, and you've made it to Week Four, so let's keep going, right? This week will be challenging as we prepare to face the anger for the first time. Why are you angry? Be honest and raw. After all, it's only you and me here.

Write out your anger below.

_____

_____

_____

_____

_____

_____

_____

_____

REMEMBER THIS WEEK

You're ALLOWED to be angry. You have every right to be angry. Let the anger flow out of your fingertips while journaling this week. Let the anger spill out from your pen or pencil.

When your child dies, you're either stuck in the past where they once lived, or you're stuck in the future because it looks so daunting and impossible. Often, we need the caring reminder to stay in the present moment. ***List the things that you're doing to stay in the present moment today and this week.***

-
-
-
-
-
-
-
-
-
-

REMEMBER THIS WEEK

Use this week as a reflection period. Make sure to be conscious about being in the present moment. Plant your feet on the ground, focus on your breathing, close your eyes, and as crazy as it sounds, try to color a picture.

I hope that you're feeling a little more rested from last week. We took a week to relax and stay in the present moment, but now it's time to get back to work because this is going to be another challenging week.

Think of what your plans were for you and your child and how you pictured your life together. How did you think it was going to go?
Explain these plans below.

_____

_____

_____

_____

_____

_____

_____

_____

_____

_____

REMEMBER THIS WEEK

It's okay to mourn the plans that you made for your life together. It's okay to have made these plans, and you didn't fail by not fulfilling them. Now reread these sentences over and over again.

Take a deep breath.

Did you know that according to Hebrew numerology, the number seven is considered perfect? In the Bible, it shows the number seven as a number of completeness. It's the true symbol of God's work. God created the world in six days, and on the seventh day, He rested (Genesis 1-2:2). In the days of the flood, Noah led the clean animals into the ark in sets of seven pairs for each species. In Exodus 20:9-11, God set apart the seventh day as the holy Sabbath and to rest in observance of it. Jesus also spoke in seven petitions in regards to how we should pray (Matthew 6:9-13). I could go on and on, but I'll leave that to a Bible study on a different day! *This week seems most fitting, on the seventh week of this journal, to write a letter to your beloved perfect-in-your-eyes child. Really think about this. You're not writing to me, you're writing to them.*

_____

_____

_____

_____

_____

_____

_____

_____

_____

_____

REMEMBER THIS WEEK

"The Lord is close to the brokenhearted and saves those who are crushed in spirit." Psalm 34:18.

Looking back on the past eight weeks, who has been there for you? How have they shown support? Who could you call at any hour of the night?
Share your gratitude for them below:

_____

_____

_____

_____

_____

_____

_____

_____

_____

_____

REMEMBER THIS WEEK

Take some time as you reflect on who has been there to support you and simply thank them for loving you. It's not an easy job to stand by someone through their grief. Although your job is way harder by having to rummage through all your emotions, their job is difficult as well, but in a different way.

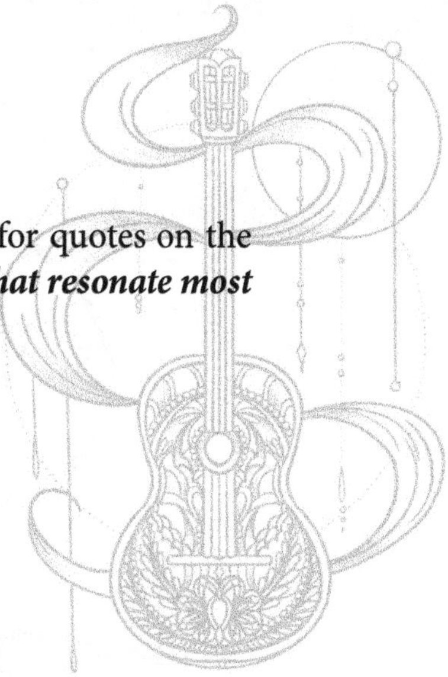

If you're like me, you've probably scoured the internet for quotes on the topic of child loss. If you haven't, try it. *List the quotes that resonate most with you and warm your spirit below:*

-
-
-
-
-
-
-
-
-
-

REMEMBER THIS WEEK

Some quotes are helpful, and some quotes are hurtful. Be mindful of yourself and your vulnerability right now. Return to this page throughout the week to gain additional encouragement and re-encouragement.

Music is good for the soul. Are there any songs that you've been listening to on repeat? *Write the songs below. Feel free to include some of the lyrics that jump out to you and sing to your grieving heart.*

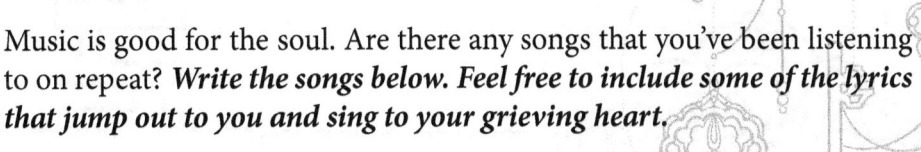

-
-
-
-
-
-
-
-
-
-
-

REMEMBER THIS WEEK

Feel free to revisit this page throughout the upcoming weeks and add to it. Write the artists' names as well so that you can look up the lyrics years from now.

If your child had a bedroom that they left behind, and you haven't brought yourself to go into their room yet, that's okay. Everyone is on a different timeline with their grief. There is no need to feel rushed.

This is the week where we focus on a list of the special items of your child's that are still here. Where should they go now? You could keep the items the same and not move them, or give your family or close friends something that reminds them of your child. You could also give some items to your child's friends or neighbors, anyone that your child was close to. But it's ultimately your decision. *List some items that were precious to your child and who you think your child would choose for each individual item:*

-
-
-
-
-
-
-
-

REMEMBER THIS WEEK

If this task seems too challenging, set it down and practice breathing instead. Feel free to return to this page in the future when you're ready. Think of how much you can bless someone else just by giving them something that was your child's.

Write down your most treasured memory of your child:

REMEMBER THIS WEEK
Spend time coming back to this treasured memory. Try to recall the curves of your child's face, how their voice sounded, how their laugh radiated, etc.

When grief of this magnitude happens, some people are bound to be, for lack of a better word, idiots. Some people literally have no idea how to react to trauma and grief. I say quite often in our support groups that grief brings out the best in people and the worst in people. So, this week, we address the stupid things that people have said and/or done. ***Write the stupid things that people have said to you.*** Heck, you can even write the names of the stupid people. By doing this exercise, you're allowing yourself to get those negative emotions and comments OUT of your body and mind and onto paper. Imagine this paper as glue: once it's written out completely on this page, you can't pick it back up in your mind to stew on or think about. Or perhaps, most of all, you can't pick it back up to believe.

_____

_____

_____

_____

_____

_____

_____

_____

_____

_____

_____

_____

_____

_____

_____

_____

_____

_____

_____

_____

_____

_____

_____

REMEMBER THIS WEEK

Anger is so powerful, but so is Grace. You're allowed to separate yourself from the people that you used to hang out with before this loss. You're allowed to recluse if you feel that you need to. Giving grace to those that don't understand grief isn't for them, but for you. It doesn't tie that anger to your feet like anchors and chains. Choose to forgive them and keep focusing on what matters. Your child. Your grief. ***If you're still mad after this exercise, try crossing their names out once with a pen.***

Fourteen weeks have gone by, and I know that they have felt like an eternity. You have put in some HARD work up to this point. This week is a time of self-reflection. ***List the self-care practices in your life right now. If you don't have any, START some now.***

-
-
-
-
-
-
-
-
-
-

REMEMBER THIS WEEK

Self-care looks different for each person. For some it could be anything from getting a massage, exercising, spending time in this journal, coloring, sleeping, taking a walk, seeing a therapist, practicing your breathing. And for others it could be something as simple as taking a shower or brushing your teeth. Whatever you decide, make some time for yourself. It's essential.

Rejuvenating a space in your house can be remarkable. And it may seem redundant, but it helps to not let the mind get attached to things. ***Try listing some ways that you can change your space around.*** This could be in your child's room, or another part of your living space that's impactful. If you haven't already, you could also utilize this week to make some sort of memorial for your child. This can be a place where you go to feel closer to them.

-
-
-
-
-
-
-
-
-

REMEMBER THIS WEEK

Your feelings are not attached to things. Although it may seem super challenging, choose something to change this week and notice how your mood is impacted. I decided to regift some of Bo's Mickey Mouse decorations using this mantra.

List your best qualities as a parent. Sounds simple, right? Turns out, we're our worst critic. **_Write your best qualities below:_**

-
-
-
-
-
-
-
-
-
-
-

REMEMBER THIS WEEK

You are not your failures. Return to this page to remind yourself what good qualities you have as a parent. Feel free to add to this list throughout the year as you realize more of the incredible qualities that you possess.

Have you heard of signs from heaven? What are some signs that remind you of your child? *Write them below:*

-
-
-
-
-
-
-
-
-
-

REMEMBER THIS WEEK

Feel free to use this page as a record keeper. Store all the times that you saw a special sign that reminded you of your child. For some parents, it's pennies or cardinals; other parents see butterflies or dragonflies. When you see these things out in the world, say your child's name out loud. Thank them for the gift.

So, you're having a bad day, or even a bad week. Did you get out of bed today? Did you get out of bed at all this week? You probably didn't want to, and that's okay. ***What are some things that make you feel better? What are some things that cheer you up? Write them below:***

-
-
-
-
-
-
-
-
-
-

REMEMBER THIS WEEK

Did you know that your Joy is never really gone? Because Joy comes from the Lord. And if He is the only one that can give Joy, then there's no way anyone can steal it. Come back to this page throughout the next couple of weeks as a reminder whenever you need it!

We've been together for nineteen weeks now. And I've only tiptoed around the area of spiritual growth. For some, this week might be a challenging one. ***Write your letter to God below, keeping in mind that He is a BIG God and He can take ALL of your anger and anguish. Lay it at His feet:***

_____
_____
_____
_____
_____
_____
_____
_____
_____
_____
_____
_____
_____
_____

_____

_____

_____

_____

_____

_____

_____

_____

_____

_____

_____

_____

_____

REMEMBER THIS WEEK

In order to properly process this grief, you need to understand that you have lost control. It was taken from you, whether you surrendered that control or not. God hears your cries in the middle of the night. He knows what's happening. He's not blind to your agony. Don't be modest, because now is not the time. Let that anger towards Him out.

After last week, I feel that we need to try and take it easy this week. While you're trying to kick your feet up for some R&R (rest and recovery), *I want you to write down any dreams that you've had in the past twenty weeks of and about your child.*

REMEMBER THIS WEEK

Dreams are a way that God can communicate to you. Every dream is a gift from heaven. If you haven't dreamt of your child yet, don't worry, it's coming. Feel free to leave this week's entry blank until you dream of them, or you can write about what you hope to see in your dreams.

Let's talk more about your child. Did your child have a name? Why did you choose that name? Does their name have a meaning? *Write about your child's name below:*

REMEMBER THIS WEEK

Say your child's name. It's been twenty-one weeks and you may feel that people are starting to forget. You have permission to say your child's name every day, but especially this week!

Week Twenty-Two

Face your trauma. Grief is hard work, remember? *Write out your most traumatic hours below. Don't get discouraged if you can't finish this one. We will address this again later.*

REMEMBER THIS WEEK
You are NOT your trauma. This happened TO you, but it is NOT you.

Last week was hard, so this week we are going to focus on motivation. ***What are some things that help keep you motivated?***

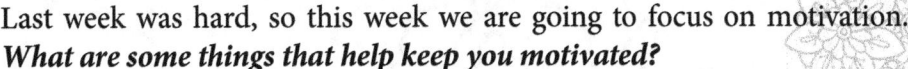

-
-
-
-
-
-
-
-
-
-

REMEMBER THIS WEEK

Motivation is good, but try not to be discouraged if it runs away as quickly as it came. Your body is enduring trauma. Your brain is already tired. Come back here when you remember additional things that help motivate you and jot them down.

Week Twenty-Four

It's so essential to find support when moving through the grieving process. ***What types of support do you need at this moment? What supports do you have? Write them below:***

REMEMBER THIS WEEK

This answer is completely different for everyone. Some parents need space and alone time, others need a therapist or a psychiatrist. Some seek support groups to surround themselves with other parents who understand, and some just want ice cream as a support. As long as you're not doing harm to yourself or anyone else, any way that you can get that support is valid.

Think of an affirmation that has taken you to this point. Do you have one? If so, what is it? If you don't have an affirmation that has been something that you speak out loud to yourself daily, then let's come up with one now. For example: Any I AM statements, like "I am loved, I am enough, I am safe." Or "I can do this, this is not my fault, I will survive this, I did not deserve this." **Write your affirmation below:**

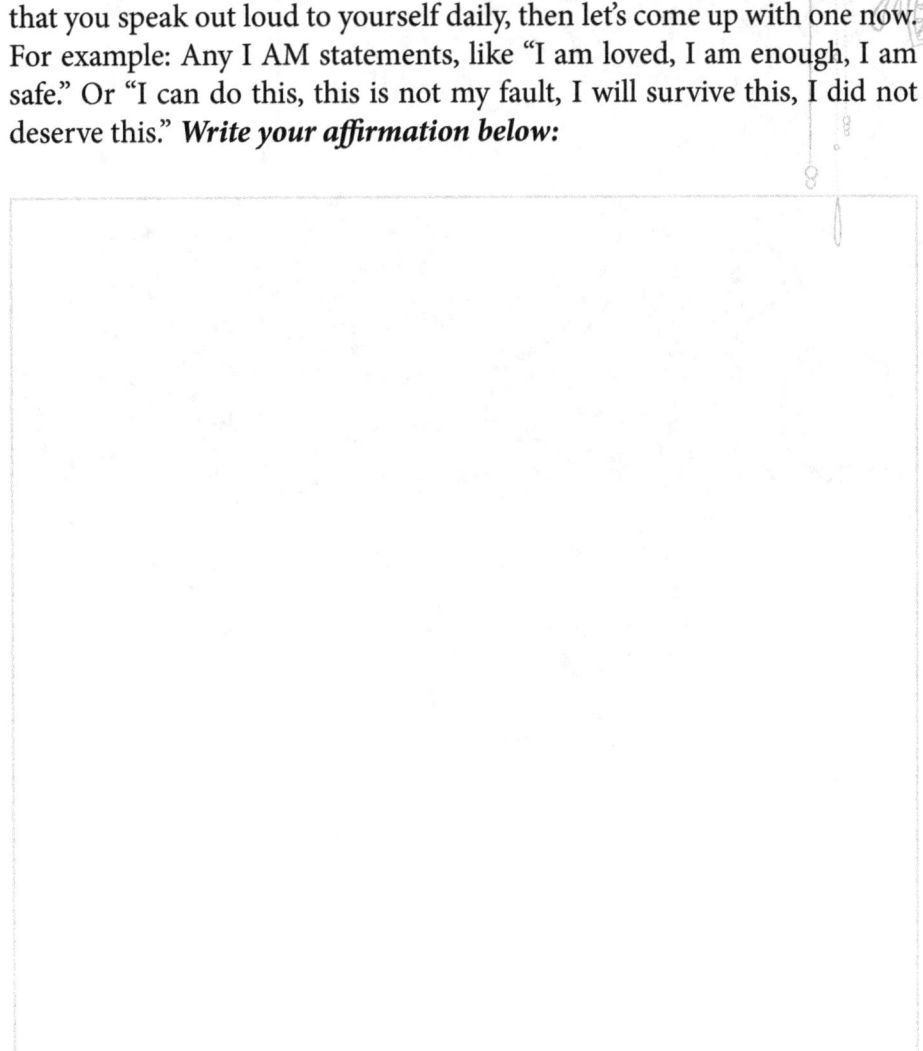

REMEMBER THIS WEEK

Come back to this page on your worst days. Read your affirmation repeatedly. Until you begin to believe it again.

We've been together for just about six months. And throughout this time, I've brought up my love for Jesus but once. I've mentioned that Joy comes from the Lord, and I hope that you won't take me at my word when you read that. I would encourage you to look it up. And while you're at it, search throughout the Bible to find ONE verse that sticks out to you.

Write it below:

_____

_____

_____

_____

_____

_____

_____

_____

_____

_____

REMEMBER THIS WEEK

"Weeping may stay overnight, but there is joy in the morning." Psalm 30:5. Even if you've never read a Bible before, there's no harm in following this journal prompt through to its entirety, right?

This week is going to be about things that have been left unsaid. Whether they are to your child, to your spouse, or to that one person who hasn't understood your grieving process since the very beginning, ***write your things that have been left unsaid below:***

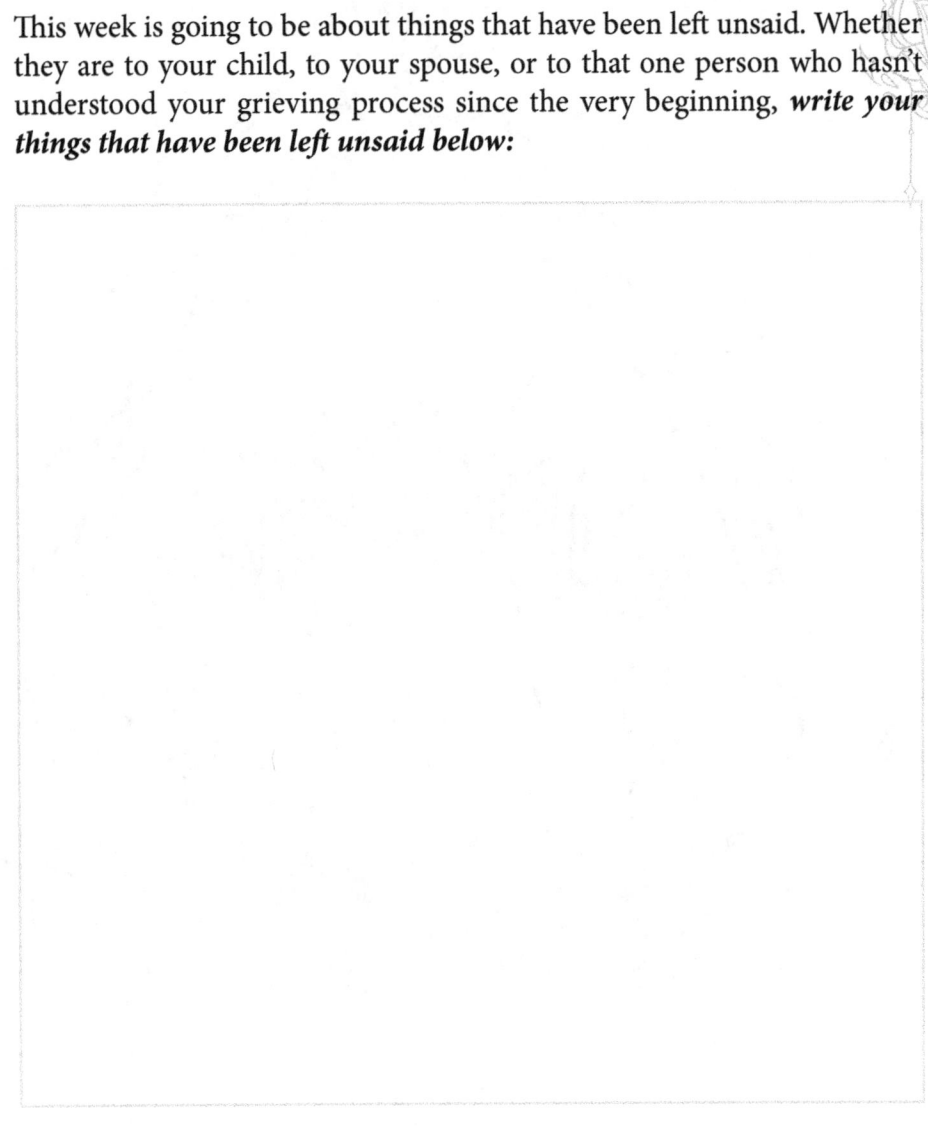

REMEMBER THIS WEEK

Prepare for a hurricane of emotions. Unbottling the things that have been left unsaid to whoever they may be can provoke a lot of anger and hurt feelings. Remember to breathe and count to ten slowly in your mind. Let go of the anger with every exhale you make. Refer to Week Thirteen for help.

Week Twenty-Eight

Let's get crafty.
List the things that you want to make for your child below:

-
-
-
-
-
-
-
-
-
-
-

REMEMBER THIS WEEK

This list can be anything. A photo album full of treasured photos, a handmade card, a letter, a blanket, a scrapbook. The options are endless when it comes to a parent wanting to make things that are extremely special for their child. Come back to this list throughout the year and make it a goal to complete at least two of these items.

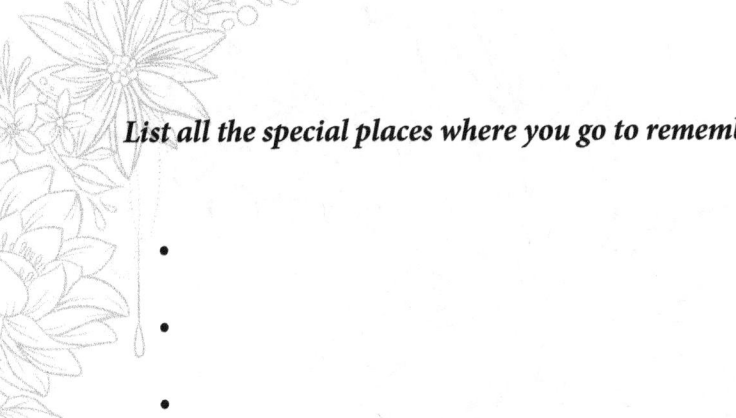

List all the special places where you go to remember your child:

-
-
-
-
-
-
-
-
-
-
-

REMEMBER THIS WEEK

If you feel like you don't have any special places that you go to, remember that it could be right at your kitchen table. Try to go to at least one of the places on your list this week.

The trauma piece is still there. Thirty weeks have passed, and you probably still remember every millisecond that took place that day. It may sound bizarre, but that is what makes you a good parent. You loved this little being of yours so much that your brain has permanently remembered the most debilitating pain of your life. After establishing that you're in a safe place, let's revisit that trauma together. Write down the date that your child passed away and then take a deep breath. ***Write down the events that took place the day that your child ventured Home.***

_____

_____

_____

_____

_____

_____

_____

_____

_____

_____

_____

REMEMBER THIS WEEK
Say it with me: This is NOT your fault. You did EVERYTHING that you could. Let this be your mantra this week.

Write down all that you remember from your child's funeral. Don't be alarmed if you cannot remember a lot of it. Your brain is built with a protection mechanism, so if you're feeling upset with yourself because you're unable to recall every detail, try to give yourself grace because your mind has been working overtime on protecting you. ***Take a deep breath and revisit the day of the funeral. Write down all the details that you can remember:***

_____
_____
_____
_____
_____
_____
_____
_____
_____
_____
_____
_____

REMEMBER THIS WEEK

If you didn't have a funeral for your child, use this spot to record ways that you have honored their memory.

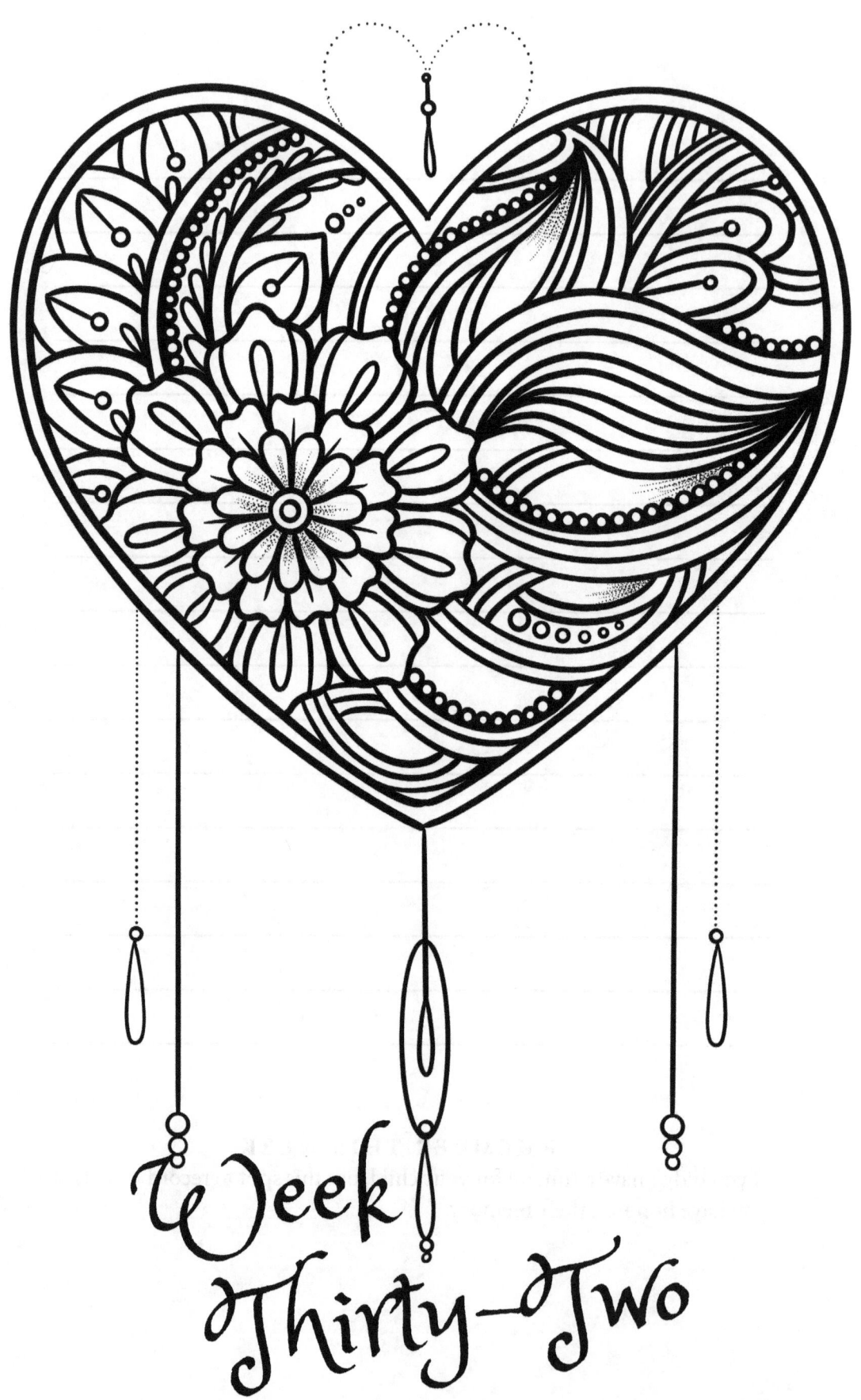

Week Thirty-Two

List five favorite things about yourself:

-

-

-

-

-

REMEMBER THIS WEEK

As I mentioned in Week Sixteen, we're often our worst critic. It may take you all week, but write five things that you truly love about yourself. Then take those five things, write them down on a piece of paper, and put it on your bathroom mirror because you're amazing and loved very much.

Because we're human beings, we reevaluate everything hundreds and thousands of times over. You've probably already thought about this, but let's write it down on paper. ***Write out what you would have done differently, if you had the chance:***

_____

_____

_____

_____

_____

_____

_____

_____

_____

_____

_____

_____

_____

_____

_____

_____

_____

_____

_____

_____

_____

_____

_____

_____

_____

_____

_____

_____

REMEMBER THIS WEEK

Obviously, all our answers would be "If I could have done something differently, I would've saved you." But I challenge you to go beyond that. Further than the day that your child passed away. What else would you have done differently?

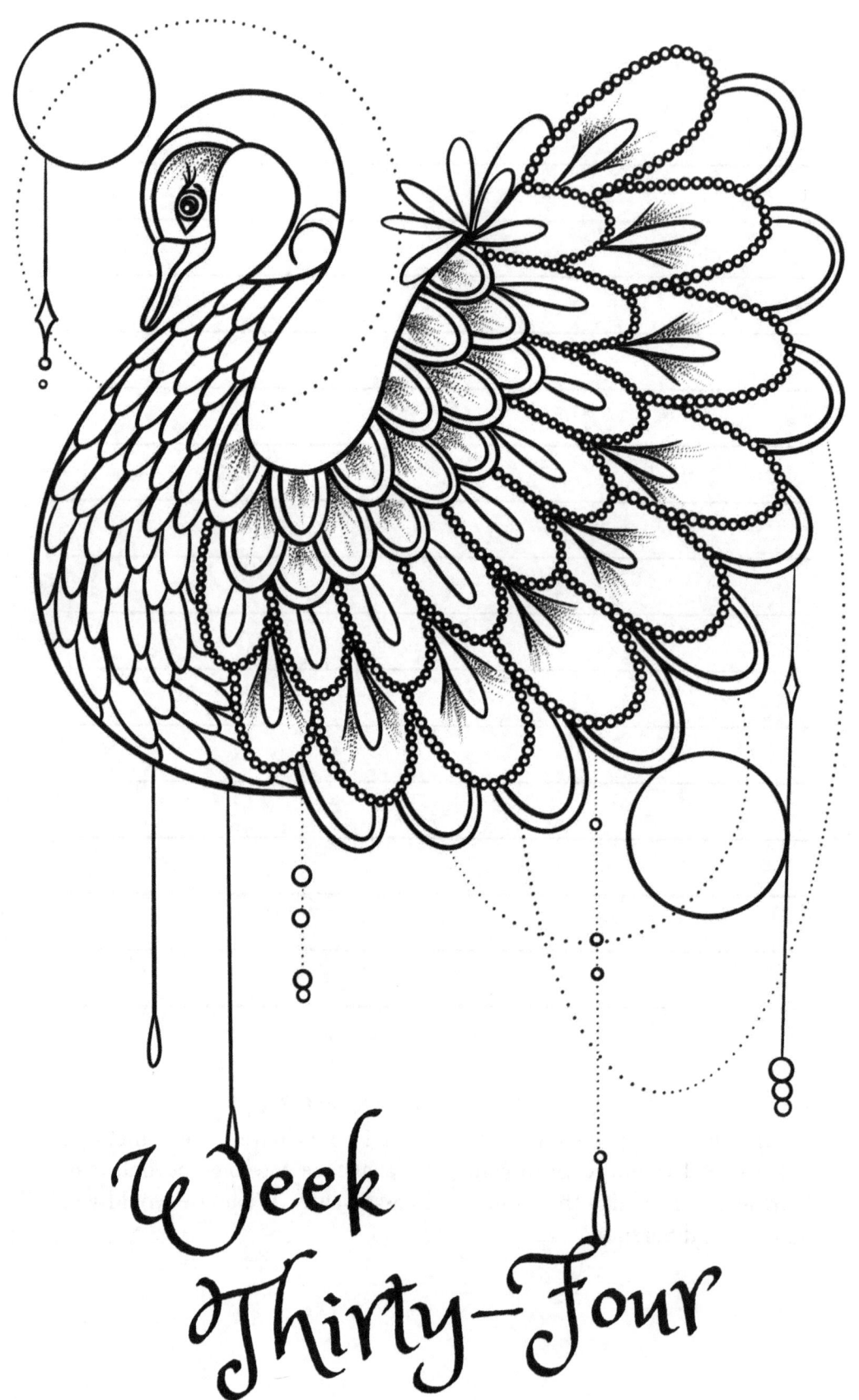

Week Thirty-Four

Time for some more self-love and self-help. This week, concentrate on the things that make you feel rejuvenated. Think of things that make you feel healthy, that make your heart happy, and that make your soul smile. What are they? Maybe it's being outdoors or writing. **Whatever makes your soul happy, write them below:**

-
-
-
-
-
-
-
-
-
-

REMEMBER THIS WEEK

Make a conscious effort to take one or two of these things that make you feel good and implement them into your everyday life. Starting now.

List your triggers:

-
-
-
-
-
-
-
-
-
-
-
-

REMEMBER THIS WEEK

Being honest about what triggers you is essential to your grieving process. The work that you're putting in now is going to show years from now. Take some serious time to reflect on the true triggers of your loss.

Week Thirty-Six

List the things that you miss most about your child:

-
-
-
-
-
-
-
-
-
-
-

REMEMBER THIS WEEK

This list could go on forever. I know that, and you know that. But take your time adding things that you miss about your beloved. It may come flooding in at one time, or it may take a few days to really ponder what you miss.

Write a farewell letter to who you were before your loss:

_____

_____

_____

_____

_____

_____

_____

_____

_____

_____

_____

_____

_____

_____

_____

_____

REMEMBER THIS WEEK
By now, you've probably realized that grief changes people. You are not the same person that you were before your child passed away. And that's okay. You're not meant to be the same person. If you were the same person, what would that say about the amount of love that you had for your child? You're meant to be changed. Forever. But it doesn't have to be a bad thing. You grow, you wilt, you grow.

The Blame Game is dangerous. It's a lot like grief. If not dealt with correctly, it can spread like wildfire throughout your heart and soul. Who do you blame for your loss? *Write and explain below:*

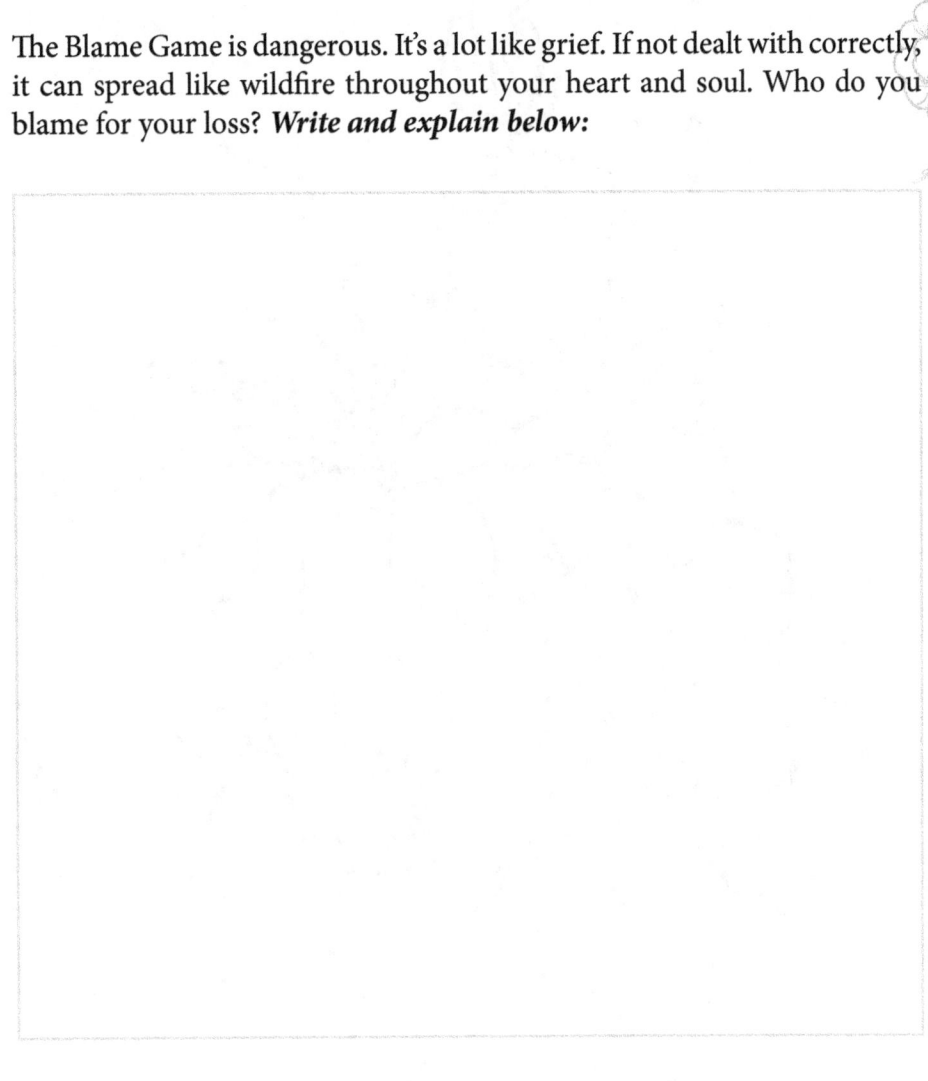

REMEMBER THIS WEEK

This week is tough because blame is never a good thing to hold on to. Whether it's your spouse, yourself, or God, it's essential to get those feelings out so that your loss can be properly dealt with. And remember, return to previous weeks to reflect on what anger does to the heart. Take a deep breath, and let this blame go. It will not bring your child back. If you see a therapist, bring this page with you to the next therapy session.

Write down some ways that you can honor your child.

-
-
-
-
-
-
-
-
-
-

REMEMBER THIS WEEK

Parents have thought of so many ways to honor their children. If their child was in the hospital, some parents donate essentials to hospitals. If their child was an animal lover, some parents give back to their local humane society. If their child was like mine, some parents go out and start an organization in their memory. These ways will all be different, but that's a good thing! Take action! Find out ways to make this happen in memory of your child.

Week Forty

Nine months. Nine months we've been together, and you have put in some major work so far. You're taking strides in the grief world to take your life back in a different way. Last week, we talked about honoring your child and doing something great in their memory. ***This week, I'm challenging you to write down a list of things that make you excited.***

-
-
-
-
-
-
-
-
-

REMEMBER THIS WEEK

You're allowed to smile again. You're allowed to feel that joy that comes from God. Your child is watching and cheering you on. I promise that they don't want to see you miserable. Can you imagine how proud you would make them if you decided to help make this world a better place in their honor?

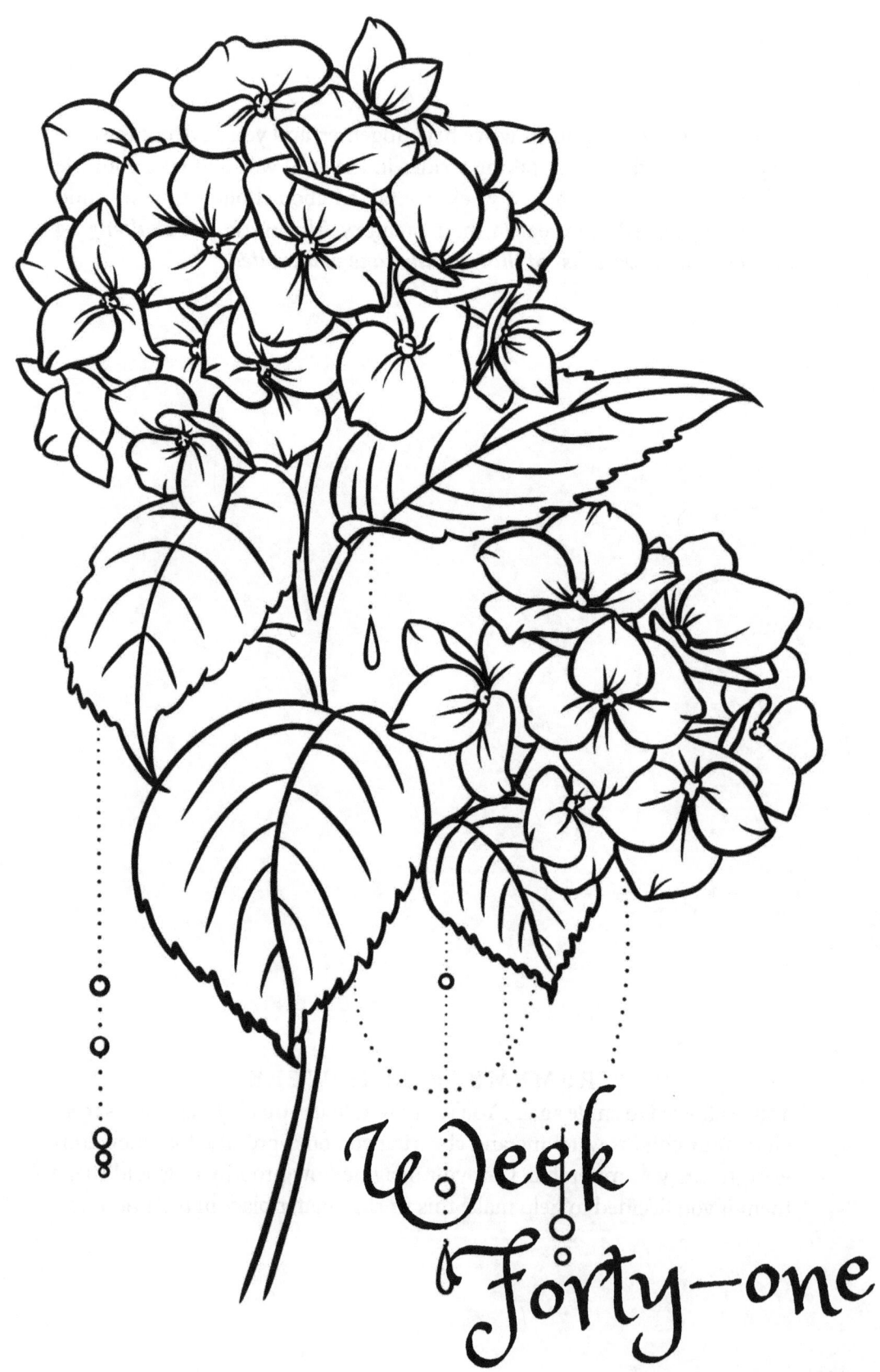

Trauma. I'm sure that the horrors of the day your child left this earthly place haunt you. It haunted me for months, maybe years. Until I realized that I couldn't control it. Although I was Bo's mommy, I couldn't protect him from everything like I promised him. I had to realize that I was powerless in this life, and that was a real tough pill for me to swallow because I was the type of person that needed to control everything. **List the things that you forgive yourself for:**

-
-
-
-
-
-
-
-

REMEMBER THIS WEEK

When revisiting this trauma section of your brain, the agitation might stir back up. Try to take deep breaths and focus on some self-care exercises to allow your mind to rest on the idea that someone higher is in control. You can forgive yourself for thinking you were always in control, for "letting" this happen, and so much more. The guilt that you have isn't yours to carry. Lay it down at the feet of the only One who can handle it.

Week Forty-Two

Write down your new favorite song lyrics below:

REMEMBER THIS WEEK

Music can be so healing. Allow yourself to listen to many different genres of music and truly listen to how the lyrics play into your life right now. Come back to this page throughout the rest of the year.

Grief brings up a whole mess of emotions. Often, it's the anxiety the week or two before the actual holidays that are the worst, but the holidays themselves are often excruciating. ***Describe how you plan on handling the holidays:***

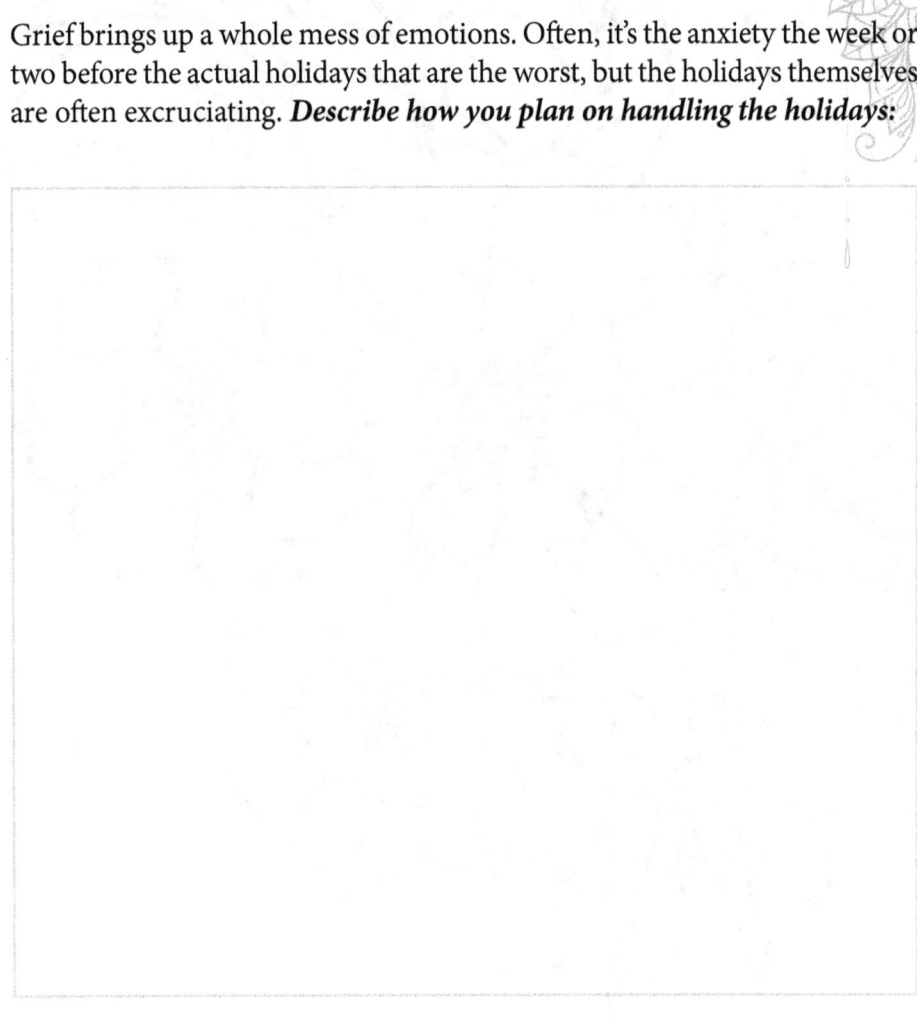

REMEMBER THIS WEEK

Anything that is not going to harm you or anyone else is okay. I've seen parents take a trip to Mexico and boycott the holidays completely, and I've seen parents invite their families over so that they don't have to be alone through the holidays. I've also seen parents hermit themselves in their homes until the holidays were over. All of these options are okay! It's different for everyone. But planning a course of action is essential to get through the grief roller coasters.

Jot down a few things that make you feel the most at peace:

-
-
-
-
-
-
-
-
-
-

REMEMBER THIS WEEK
Give yourself space. Consciously take time away from social media and allow yourself to figure out what makes you feel most at peace.

Think of the things that people have said that have drawn comfort to your heart. *Write those things below:*

REMEMBER THIS WEEK

Think back to the first few weeks into your loss. Were there people that really offered some helpful support and encouraging words?

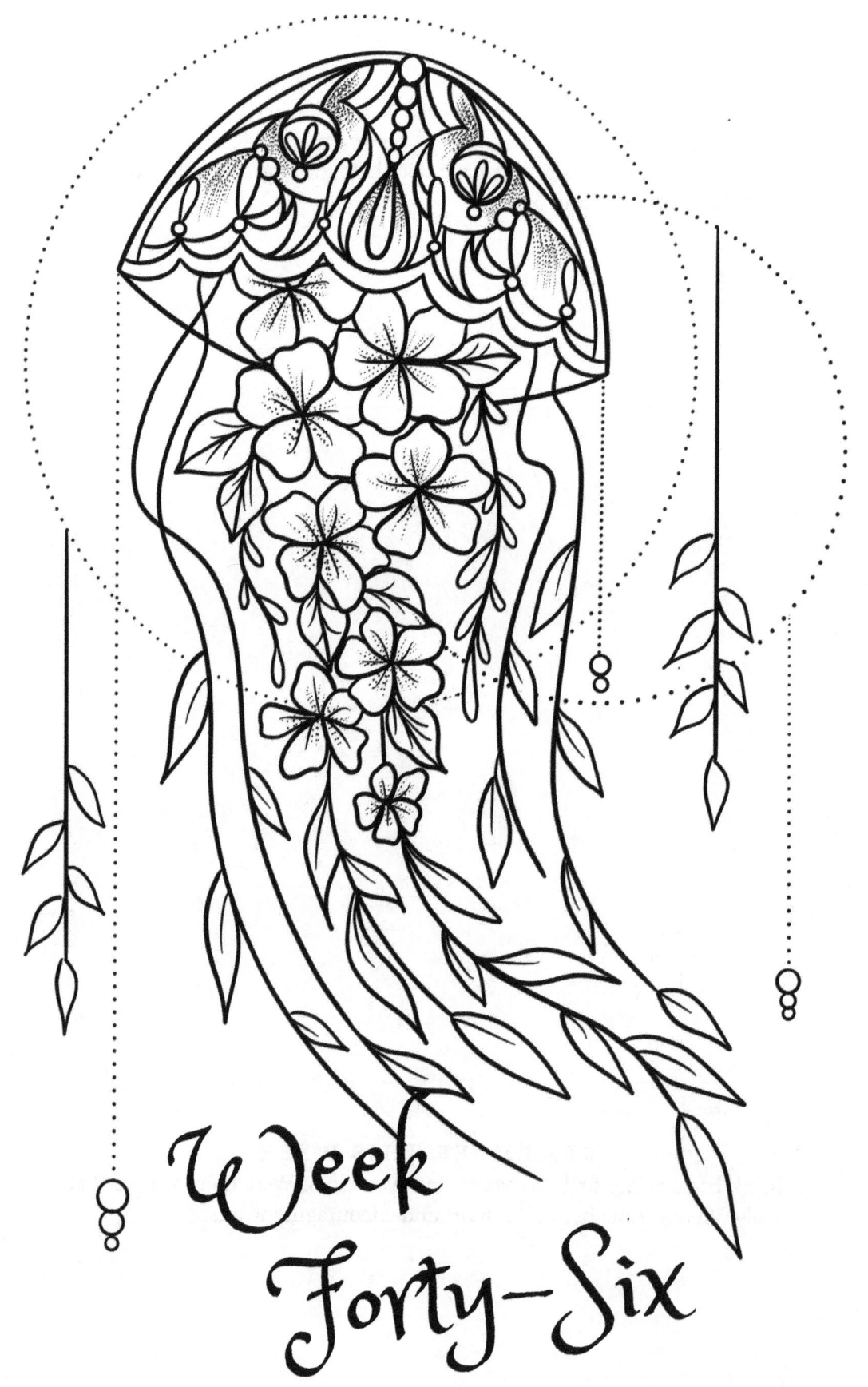

The dreaded "firsts" are so hard. ***List the firsts that you have had to experience and explain how they are different from last year.***

-
-
-
-
-
-
-

REMEMBER THIS WEEK

The firsts are only here for a season. They do not last forever. *"There is a time for everything, and a season for every activity under the heavens: a time to be born and a time to die, a time to plant and a time to uproot, a time to kill and a time to heal, a time to tear down and a time to build, a time to weep and a time to laugh, a time to mourn and a time to dance, a time to scatter stones and a time to gather them, a time to embrace and a time to refrain from embracing, a time to search and a time to give up, a time to keep and a time to throw away, a time to tear and a time to mend, a time to be silent and a time to speak, a time to love and a time to hate, a time for war and a time for peace." Ecclesiastes 3:1-8*

At this moment, write down your greatest comfort(s) that you have:

REMEMBER THIS WEEK

Early on in my grief, I had to recognize that my son was not tied to physical things. Things that once brought me comfort in the beginning weeks were not giving me that same comfort now. For example, I collected Mickey Mouse items from others because he loved watching Mickey. Weeks passed by before I started to realize that I was trying to chase the feeling of him in other things that weren't even his. They were strangers'. But it's what got me through that season. What are you holding on to that you can let go of? Try to evaluate your greatest comforts, or better yet, try to combine them into an ultimate self-care day!

Search your gratitudes. These past eleven months, you have changed beyond measure. There have been some overwhelming, soul-crushing days. But there are also days that you can reflect on and be grateful for. ***What are you grateful for? Write it below:***

-
-
-
-
-
-
-
-
-
-

REMEMBER THIS WEEK

Gratitude isn't that hard to find. It could be something as simple as the barista at the coffee shop asking you how your day has been. You can be grateful while still grieving. It's okay to allow those two worlds to coexist.

I've mentioned in previous weeks that you've come a long way. You've put in such a huge amount of hard work. This week, think about all the obstacles in your mind that you have overcome. ***Write down your accomplishments, whether they are big or small:***

-
-
-
-
-
-
-
-
-

REMEMBER THIS WEEK

You have taken strides this week. I'm so proud of you. Come back to this page throughout the week and add to your accomplishments. You'll think of big and small accomplishments, but there is no accomplishment too small that cannot be noted. Keep going.

Reflect on the last fifty weeks that we have had together. Think about all the articles and books that you have come across on this grief journey. What stands out? ***Write down all the books or articles that have helped you grieve:***

-
-
-
-
-
-
-
-
-
-
-

REMEMBER THIS WEEK

I encourage you to go back to your favorite articles and books and write down the authors' names so you can turn back to them years from now.

This will be our last time revisiting the trauma piece of your life together. You and I have grown close over the past fifty-one weeks. And I'm so proud of you. Center yourself on the ground by placing your feet flat on the floor. Revisit the trauma of your child's last day on earth. What's different about this time? ***You've gone back to this trauma thousands of times. But this time is different. How?***

REMEMBER THIS WEEK

Revisit Weeks 13, 22, 30, and 41. You've put some real trauma work in. You've rolled up your sleeves and put the work in to heal. Think about how your outlook on this trauma has changed over the weeks.

Week Fifty-Two

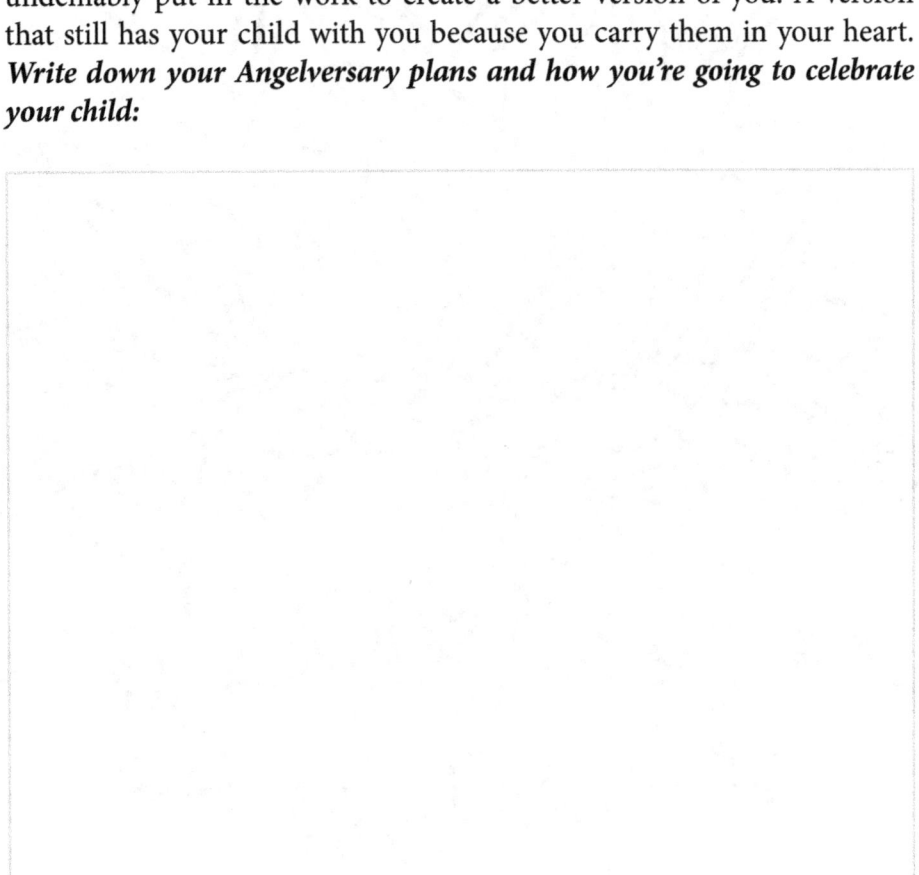

The Angelversary. This is the final week that we have together. You've undeniably put in the work to create a better version of you. A version that still has your child with you because you carry them in your heart. ***Write down your Angelversary plans and how you're going to celebrate your child:***

REMEMBER THIS WEEK

Whatever plans you have for your child's Angelversary are okay. You can have people over, be alone, plant a tree or a flower, release balloons, go visit them at their grave, have a party in their memory, etc. Whatever you decide, make sure it's right for you and for them. You're at the one-year mark. And I know that most of it will seem like a blur, but because you took the time to document your year, years from now you will be able to gain some perspective on exactly how you made it through. Take some time this week to reflect and reread some of your previous writings.

What Now?

You did it. One year of walking through child loss. Together. You accomplished this, and I am so proud of you. I want you to know that on the days that you don't feel like you're enough or you're questioning if you're worthy or not, you are. You did not deserve this. You did not choose this. But your child lives in you. Tucked right inside your heart, safe and sound. Please be gentle with yourself as you've approached the one-year anniversary of your beloved's passing. Honor all of the feelings that come. It is so important that you remember to replenish the tools in your grieving toolbox and constantly reflect back to this book if you need any encouragement. You, my friend, are a warrior. You can do this. And, perhaps most importantly, you are not alone.

. . .

www.ingramcontent.com/pod-product-compliance
Lightning Source LLC
LaVergne TN
LVHW061253060426
835507LV00017B/2049